After the Night Rain
Haiku

After the Night Rain

Haiku

James G. Brueggemann

DANKWORTH

PUBLISHING

After the Night Rain: Haiku
© 2014 James G. Brueggemann

Some of the haiku in this book were first published in *Dragonfly*, *Japan Air Lines Anthology of Haiku by People of the United States and Canada*, *Leanfrog* and *Modern Haiku*, whose editors are gratefully acknowledged. Some are reprinted with permission from *Group Practice Journal* ©*1987*, *American Medical Group Association, September/October 1987*.

Cover Art and Illustrations © 2014 Kaori Mitsushima

ISBN-13: 978-0-9855676-2-0
ISBN-10: 0-9855676-2-7
Dankworth Publishing, LLC
Oberlin, Ohio USA
www.dankworthpublishing.com

Manufactured in the United States of America

For Carolyn,
who smiled at me

Haiku are rooted in the concept of place. They are snapshots of personal experience, emotional instants, images of nature mirroring daily life. In them, dual observations may be connected by a single thread.

—James G. Brueggemann

Contents

Duluth and Then Some   1

Making Rounds   23

The Way Home   31

Bear Hill Cabin   49

Grandfather Haiku   65

In the Lowcountry   77

Duluth and Then Some

Duluth, in northern Minnesota, is defined by trees and water, hills and rocks, ships and wilderness. It's urban, but not in a big way; it's Midwestern, but without the cornfields.

Winter's over:
Nanking cherries explode
In drifts of white

First spring lawnmower
Droning busily outside
Cutting dandelions

The crabapple tree –
Shedding blossoms
On two yards

Cleaning out old leaves
From under cedar bushes,
The rake scratches ice

Spring aspens
Lined up roadside:
Green in D-flat

Fresh asparagus
From a good friend's garden:
Such deep roots

Sunny morning
After spring fog:
Crows everywhere

Today's my dad's birthday
I don't remember his death year:
Spring green, glowing

Maples leaf out
On the hillside, each
With its own shadow

Ice fog crystals
Drifting through a spruce forest:
My friend's new kidney

Spring morning after church
A nun reads Sunday comics:
Black habit quivers

Holding her baby
She trots down a little hill…
Both start laughing

Until now
I had not smelled your perfume:
Sharing an umbrella

Man mowing lawn
Makes an extra pass
Near the azalea

Busy day!
Knotweed bunches
In sidewalk cracks

Moving furniture
Out of our apartment
In the rain

The feeling
Perhaps we know each other
Just never met

Selecting beach stones
For a porch fountain:
Moth alights

Eating wild spinach
From a cemetery lane:
Family tree

In an oak woods
An overgrown clearing:
Leftover lilacs

Cornfield cicadas
Shrilling in the humid breeze:
Rough leaves rattle

The little bounce
A crow gives
Upon alighting

This moment
Is why droplets hang on railings:
Two here, three there

Acres of summer grain
And this goldfinch, feeding on
A bending thistle

So brief
The carpet flattened
By a backpack

After the night rain
Crickets' conversations seem
Louder than before

I own nothing:
Just the cerulean
Of the evening sky

Calling to my mother,
Dead now a full year:
"Look, the moon!"

Silver-haired violinist
Listens, replaces his glasses,
Begins his part

Gently sloping
Summer hills:
Wife sleeping

Drifting fog
Swirls around First Lutheran Church:
The sound of handbells

Reflecting water
Covering, uncovering
Shore rock at nightfall

Ignoring
The northern lights
Counting constellations

Falling leaves,
A line of geese:
Retirement congrats

Mother and child
Part at the corner
Walking backward

Mother and daughter
Last minute primping
School bus stop

Beneath the white oak
A carpet of brown acorns:
Squirrels can't keep up

Pausing,
Little Halloween revelers
Gaze at the orange moon

Mottled fall clouds,
Geese honking overhead:
Morning newspaper

New puppy
Bites the old dog's ankles,
Eats the big dog's food

Turning forty...
Someone tosses a beer can
On my front yard

4AM bobcat howling
I stand on the front stoop:
Bare feet slowly freeze

It always snows
Around your birthday
Preparing me

Oh, it's snow
On mountain-ash berries –
Not blossoms at all!

Snow whistling
In rows across the road:
My mother's hair

Today's snow
Silently filling
Yesterday's tracks

Inside, steaming horses,
Sound of crunching fodder:
Outside, full moon

Checking his watch,
Santa outside a toy store:
Guy about my age

A new year:
Same headlights
Old news

Musing on Gandhi's words
"An indomitable will":
So many snowflakes!

Sparrows
Huddled at a chimney top
Suddenly fly off

Snowflakes
In the street lamp's glow:
Tonight, tomorrow

Long dry stalks
On the pink hydrangea –
Spring, how far away!

Making Rounds

When you make rounds in a hospital, the little things make it human. Nobody lying in bed is there by choice. Noticing chance circumstances makes the individual the universe.

Under his bed
Just for the hospital
New slippers

All her pills
In a crinkled shopping bag
And a box of raisins

Dark hospital room:
One breathing, the other –
Breathing

Turning away from
The sick woman's bedside:
Wild iris in a cup

Watching
His IV bottle being hung
Rain on the window

Hospital patient
Demands the crucifix come down:
Nurse complies, bathes him

Tomorrow's surgery:
As we talk, a sparrow hops
Along the windowsill

Old man with iris
Visiting his wife,
More frail than he

Each
Needing a laugh
They share one

Hospital visitors
Talk
Standing up

Returning
Over the hospital helipad:
A line of geese

On the nursing desk
In Intensive Care:
Fudge brownies

The Way Home

Traveling takes your soul away and gives you another one. When you are done traveling, all your souls line up. You get to choose the one you want. You can keep it forever.

The way out
Seems longer than returning:
Why is that?

Each time we leave
My Duluth pack
Ends up being thinner

Still life:
Young woman viewing a Monet
Museum guard yawning

Gauguin still life,
A pile of stuff with grapefruit:
I think I know him

Cell phone talk
Seems better by the window:
I love you, too

City winter:
Dried sidewalk salt
Far from home

Roadside saloon:
Guys at the bar talk jail time
Country western playing

I-77 mountain tunnel
Appalachian winter rain:
Dry for a minute

Foggy mountain road
Freshet tumbles into Paint Creek:
Christmas Day road trip

Medieval stone buildings:
Within them
People, things

Rhine barge
Powering through city locks:
Curve of the swan's neck

Machu Picchu:
Five hundred years of stone
And a pink flower

After morning rain
Back up on whitewashed walls
Bags of sponges

Areopagos:
Tribunal steps
Foot-polished

Semana Santa:
Darkness, float-bearers shuffling,
Orange blossom scent

Easter bells
Pealing after midnight mass:
Motor scooter buzz

Kneeling visitors
At Cathedrale Notre Dame
Taking pictures

Montmartre cellist
Backed up by a CD player:
Rounded cobblestones

Riderless
Wooden carousel horses:
Notre Dame statues

Rush hour Metro
Grandparents escorting grandson:
Handful of autumn leaves

Slit tops of crusty bread,
Split chestnuts on street braziers:
Paris cobblestones

The sound
Walking through dry leaves:
Urban relief

Pink-blossomed trees here,
Snow patches on the north face:
High road to Taos

Cedar cook-smoke,
Dog lapping snowmelt creek:
Kiva poles stick out

Old man, old woman
Admiring cherry blossoms
Again this spring

Leaving the adobe,
We latch the wooden gate:
Doves calling

Kayakers in
Rio Grande standing waves:
Multicolored helmets

Gold aspen leaves,
Douglas firs, cloudless sky:
Sweat between my shoulder blades

Purple mountains,
Gray-green scrub, yellow grass:
Hawk crossing I-10

Alongside the trailer
A log-roofed hogan:
Just the wind

Cuban woman frowns
My pesos are not like hers:
People-to-People

Horse-drawn banana cart
So different from my home:
Overhead, same clouds

Pale stalks flattened
In the red-painted cane press:
Sweet translucent juice

Spring Festival:
Lanterns swaying in the wind,
Long-life bulbs inside

Stone bench
Elderly couple visiting the pavilion
Leaning back-to-back

Sunset on Xi'an plain:
Beneath shadows of the Emperor's mound,
Winter wheat

Li River in spring:
Duck herder by a stone wall
Watches our boat

Temple eave bells,
Morning birdsong:
The mountain

Walking
Hand in hand in a new place:
Unfamiliar birds

Improbable peaks
Jut from the Guilin plain:
I should have said less

Bear Hill Cabin

In northwest Wisconsin, we built a cabin by a lake in the woods. It is a place the neighbors called Bear Hill when they were children growing up, because they usually saw black bears there. We appropriated the name. The bears are still there.

Pink, blue, gray, black
Woods drying out in spring:
Loon call

Early ice-out
Canoeing
The edge

Cluster of maples
Catches afternoon sun:
Seven thin gray stems

No help for it
In these parts of the year:
Exuberance

Finding a wood tick,
I'm creepy-crawly all over:
Sure, another one!

Stock market caving,
Sunny day, nearly calm:
Good day to plant peas

With a little rain
These bulbs will sprout –
Think so, Monsieur Cat?

Over our drifting canoe,
A whoosh-whoosh-whoosh:
Hadn't seen the eagle

Summer sunset colors
Over the lake – peach, turquoise:
Same as in winter

Dock boards
Uneven underfoot:
Watching fireworks

Outdoor symphony
On a sultry summer night:
Dragonfly-wing breeze

Rain on the roof,
Favorite tunes playing:
I am just a child

Refrigerator
Hums after a power cut:
Loons call each other

Early morning dark,
Deer breaks a twig in the woods:
Guess I'll turn over

Outboard across the lake,
Mayfly hatch overhead:
Inside, Bocelli

Oozing from
Red pine bark:
Summer heat

This morning
When I awoke the third time
The crows were calling

Grating parmesan,
A little pile gets larger:
Is it enough?

Mushrooms
Clean after rain:
Myself

In a glass dish, blooms
Fallen from the begonia:
Floating clouds

August half-moon:
Black squirrel plops green acorns
Onto our deck

Lake cooling
After a wide-open summer:
A single red leaf

Bringing in the dock
Remembering summer
One piece at a time

Turning autumn leaves
Into the compost pile:
I can't wait for spring!

Boat-lift on shore:
At one corner
A forget-me-not

So cold and wet
It could be autumn or spring:
But the leaves

World Trade Center down
Civilization at war
Ducks migrating

Presidential debates,
A cloudy, windy autumn:
Nuthatch flits toward bugs

Watching red pines
Swaying in a strong wind –
Not all together

First time
Mailing an absentee ballot:
Where's that bird going?

November's here:
Gray sky, cold wind, thin trees —
But it's October

This haiku journal,
Whichever pocket it's in--
Curve of my body

A single crow
Flaps silently through snowfall
Toward dark woods

I'm a little late
Loading wood into the stove:
One glowing coal

Grandfather Haiku

Being a grandparent means you have lived long enough to see it happen. The rest of the years are up to you.

My grandson,
Where is his life now?
Stoplight turns green

Second birthday:
Following his new toy
Older boys try it out

Pelican feather
Caught between beach rocks:
Two year old girl

Wild cherry blossoming
In the middle of our garden:
Grandchildren en route

One-year-old
Tossing kitchen pans:
He'll grow out of it

Of all the grandkids
Who likes the spiciest food?
The little one

Just off the highway,
Bedrock scoured by glaciers:
Children's fingers

Bean seeds, so pale,
Planted by grandchildren:
The waiting

Shoulder nudge:
"Grandpa, can we go fishing?"
What time is it?

Kids' lines all tangled:
Are we fishing for a meal
Or are we fishing?

Such a small fish!
But there's a yellow pail
In the boat

Her violin lesson
In the historic mansion:
New plastic signage

In the back yard
Kids' garden, mom's garden:
Such sweet carrots!

Seventieth birthday
Thought I could escape
But the candles

Completely rained out,
We sit inside the whole day
Exploring the interior

So many emotions:
I meant to say something --
Wasn't important

Here we are, grandparents!
How will they look ahead?
The chaos

Bedtime stories
The night before leaving:
Books piled on their beds

Time to return home
Dropping them off at the airport:
Morning mist

After they're gone,
Washing windows:
Leave the fingerprints

In the Lowcountry

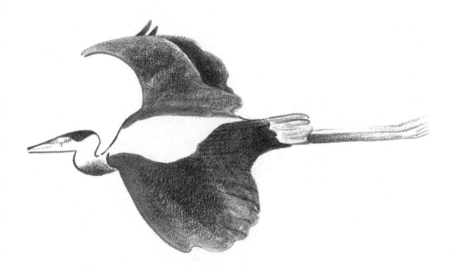

South Carolina. Marsh. Pluff mud. Oyster clusters. Live oaks and Spanish moss. Church choir and community. Camellias and Carolina jessamine. Welcome.

At the marsh today
A new plank over the creek:
Deer print in the path

Egret's feathers
Blown backward by the wind:
Yellow beak, yellow eye

Rainy day walkers
Repopulate the mall:
White sneakers, white hair

Spreading pine straw
Around the new azalea,
Vine thorn pricks my hand

Parents in the yards,
In the streets, on cell phones:
Hallowe'en

Here for trick or treat,
Superman and the Count:
Well, maybe so

How best to balance
Cell phone, briefcase, umbrella
Now that it's raining?

I'm to sing tomorrow,
A duet with an alto:
Why am I so short?

Choir director
Pauses, looks upward, nods:
End the held note

The river's surface
Rippled by a gust of wind:
Christmas Eve

Potted basil plant
Carried inside and out:
Difficult winter

Hearing a sermon,
Reminded of a friend:
Paper clip on the floor

Blue heron
Skims afternoon traffic:
Marsh expressway

Walking through
A garden of two hundred years:
Camellia blossom drops

Bringing in the plants
Ahead of a freeze warning:
Age spots on my hands

Uprooted hickory,
Three thousand year shell midden:
Past lives, washed by rain

Yaupon holly
Crooked branches, bright berries:
Christmas letter

A wave of roses
At last, after winter's cold:
Clip just one

Flock of robins
Assembled to go north:
Order the bean seeds

Trimming dead leaves
From a huge cast-iron plant:
At the ground, small shoots

Downspout gurgle,
Mid-afternoon cloudburst:
House lights go on

Carolina jessamine:
Hiking trail by the ball park
Crack of the bat

In the fruit plate
Three tangerines, two bananas:
TV news

Reading, the door open
To my neighbor's house:
Someone sneezes

James G. Brueggemann is a physician and international volunteer. He practiced medicine in Duluth, Minnesota.

His haiku, poems and personal essays have been published in both literary and medical journals. His work was included in the anthology of the Japan Air Lines English Language Haiku Contest for 1988. In 2012, he received the *New Letters* Dorothy Churchill Cappon Prize for the Essay.

He lives with his wife in the north country of Wisconsin and the Lowcountry of South Carolina.